Greater Tha Budapest

Hungary

50 Travel Tips from a Local

Isabella Beham

Isabella Beham

Copyright © 2017 CZYK Publishing
All Rights Reserved. No part of this publication may be reproduced, including scanning and photocopying, or distributed in any form or by any means, electronic or mechanical, or stored in a database or retrieval system without prior written permission from the publisher.
Disclaimer: The publisher has put forth an effort in preparing and arranging this book. The information provided herein by the author is provided "as is". Use this information at your own risk. Consult your doctor before engaging in any medical activities. The publisher and author disclaim any liabilities for any loss of profit or commercial or personal damages resulting from the information contained in this book.

Order Information: To order this title please email lbrenenc@gmail.com or visit GreaterThanATourist.com. A bulk discount can be provided.

Cover Template Creator: Lisa Rusczyk Ed. D. using Canva.
Cover Creator: Lisa Rusczyk Ed. D.
Image: https://pixabay.com/en/budapest-chain-bridge-danube-2390541/

Lock Haven, PA
All rights reserved.
ISBN: 9781549723155

>TOURIST

Isabella Beham

BOOK DESCRIPTION

Are you excited about planning your next trip?

Do you want to try something new?

Would you like some guidance from a local?

If you answered yes to any of these questions, then this Greater Than a Tourist book is for you.

Greater than a Tourist: Budapest by Isabella Beham offers the inside scoop on Budapest. Most travel books tell you how to sightsee. Although there's nothing wrong with that, as a part of the Greater than a Tourist series, this book will give you tips from someone who lives at your next travel destination. In these pages, you'll discover local advice that will help you throughout your trip.

Travel like a local. Slow down and get to know the people and the culture of a place. By the time you finish this book, you will be eager and prepared to travel to your next destination.

Isabella Beham

TABLE OF CONTENTS

BOOK DESCRIPTION

TABLE OF CONTENTS

DEDICATION

ABOUT THE AUTHOR

HOW TO USE THIS BOOK

FROM THE PUBLISHER

WELCOME TO > TOURIST

INTRODUCTION

1. Take the Bus From the Airport

2. Don't Exchange Money at the Bank

3. Find Local Accommodations

4. Stay in Pest, Not Buda

5. Check Expat Pages for Events

6. Don't Take Just Any Cab

7. Visit the Baths

8. Go to an Outdoor Movie Screening

9. Head to the Top of Buda Castle

10. Visit Ruin Pubs

11. Go to Szimpla During the Day

12. Go Hiking in Buda

13. Visit the Beach

14. Visit Romai

15. Visit the National Szechenyi Library

16. Go to the Night Baths

17. Try Langos

18. Go Shopping on Andrassy Avenue

19. Get Brunch

20. Try Hungarian Cuisine

21. Take in the Views from Rooftop Bars

22. Walk Across all of the Bridges

23. Visit Local Designers

24. Go to a Bar on the Danube

25. Shop for Vintage Clothing

26. Visit Gozsdu Udvar

27. Explore the Jewish District

28. Go on a River Cruise

29. Try Local Wines

30. Take in the View from Fisherman's Bastion

31. Visit the Museum of Applied Arts

32. Catch a Performance at the Hungarian State Opera House

33. Take a Day Trip to Szentendre

34. Try Hungarian Spirits

35. Take the Public Boat

36. Get a Thai Massage

37. Go "Dog Watching"

38. Take an Architectural Tour

39. Stop for Coffee

40. Get Dental Work Done

41. Sit Outside at Deak

42. Visit a Teahouse

43. Take a Free Walking Tour

44. Pay Your Respect at the Holocaust Memorials

45. Buy a Map at Printa

46. Visit the Great Synagogue

47. Try Hungary's Birthday Cake

48. Shop at the Great Market Hall (Vasarcsarnok)

49. Try Traditional Hungarian Desserts

50. Don't Do it All

Top Reasons to Book This Trip

Our Story

Notes

DEDICATION

This book is dedicated to Carmen McDonald.

Isabella Beham

ABOUT THE AUTHOR

Isabella Beham is a writer who lives in Budapest, Hungary. She originally moved to Budapest for school, but decided to stay after graduating because of the beautiful scenery and easy travel to other countries.

Isabella Beham

HOW TO USE THIS BOOK

The Greater Than a Tourist book series was written by someone who has lived in an area for over three months. The goal of this book is to help travelers either dream or experience different locations by providing opinions from a local. The author has made suggestions based on their own experiences. Please do your own research before traveling to the area in case the suggested places are unavailable.

Isabella Beham

FROM THE PUBLISHER

Traveling can be one of the most important parts of a person's life. The anticipation and memories that you have are some of the best. As a publisher of the Greater Than a Tourist book series, as well as the popular 50 Things to Know book series, we strive to help you learn about new places, spark your imagination, and inspire you. Wherever you are and whatever you do I wish you safe, fun, and inspiring travel.

Lisa Rusczyk Ed. D.
CZYK Publishing

Isabella Beham

WELCOME TO > TOURIST

Isabella Beham

INTRODUCTION

If you've come to Budapest, you've probably only heard good things. There's really only good things to tell. Budapest has some of the most iconic scenery in Europe, an underrated wine scene, and a growing dedication to the arts. Between its ruin pubs and dozens of thermal springs, Budapest is truly a unique city in Europe.

Some call Budapest, "The Paris of the East." While there may be some truth to this, Budapest has a charm and ruggedness that makes it an unparalleled wonder.

If you've come to Budapest, you won't be disappointed. Take full advantage of every opportunity to revel in the beauty of the city and relax. When you leave, you'll be just another one of Budapest's adoring fans.

Isabella Beham

1. Take the Bus From the Airport

Getting from the airport to the city center can take 20-40 minutes depending on the mode of transportation. A cab ride into the city center takes about 20-30 minutes and costs roughly $20-$30. Luckily for budget travelers there's now an express bus from the airport directly to Deak Ferenc ter, the metro stop in the middle of the city center. The bus takes about 40 minutes and costs only $3.50 (900 forint).

2. Don't Exchange Money at the Bank

When I first got to Budapest, I was weary of the money changers, however I soon found that they offered rates that were much more fair than the banks for converting US dollars. If you need to take out money from an ATM though, avoid ATMs on the street and go to a bank. When given the option to accept their conversion or your bank's conversion, choose your bank's, it will still come out better, despite the conversion fee.

3. Find Local Accommodations

Hotel prices in Budapest are outrageous compared to the cost of living here. If you're coming to Budapest, rent an apartment from a local instead of staying in a hotel or hostel. You can find a luxurious apartment to rent for a few days here for around 30 dollars a night or less.

Stay on Buda Hill if you want to be near the Royal Palace, or in the Jewish District if you want to visit all of the coolest bars. If you want a luxury experience, you can find an apartment to rent with a view of the Danube for around $50 a night, sometimes even less.

4. Stay in Pest, Not Buda

Budapest is actually more like two cities split in half by the Danube river. Pest, is the city, while Buda is more of a residential area. Although Buda is beautiful and hosts several tourist attractions like Buda Castle, if you're interested in nightlife, dining, and shopping, you should find a place to stay in Pest. The most popular places to stay in Pest are party hostels and apartments in the Jewish District.

Don't neglect Buda though; cross one of Budapest's famous bridges into Buda for spectacular views, thermal baths, and hiking.

5. Check Expat Pages for Events

Budapest has a thriving international scene and expat community. Do your homework and you should find tons of events to go to while you're in Budapest from English language comedy nights to moonlit paddleboarding on the Danube.

If you're visiting Budapest in June, keep an eye out for the annual "Night of Museums." Not only are all museums in Budapest free, but they also hold unique events and performances. Plus city runs direct buses between the museums all day and night. Museum entry is also free across the city on St. Istvan Day, August 20th.

6. Don't Take Just Any Cab

If you need a cab in Budapest, it's best to call a reputable service instead of choosing the first cab off of the street. Unfortunately, there aren't discount car services apps in Budapest, but the cost of a cab ride isn't usually too expensive. For your convenience you can also download the app of one of Budapest's taxi services ahead of time. Try Fotaxi or Taxify.

7. Visit the Baths

Visiting Budapest can be a truly luxurious experience. One of the best part of Budapest are its many thermal baths all over the city, originally beloved by visiting Romans for their curative properties. Today people come to Budapest from all over the world for its magical, healing waters.

Each bath has its own unique history and architecture, some dating back to the 16th century, so don't think you can visit just one while you're in town. Visit Gellert Bath in the Hotel Gellert in Buda for Art Nouveau architectural splendors or Rudas Bath on the Danube for a rooftop pool and night bathing until 4 am.

Perhaps the most popular bath is the enormous bathing complex Szechenyi Thermal Bath. Loved for its outdoor pools and cheerful yellow color, Szechenyi sees 1 million bathers a year. Although some baths, like Rudas have male or female only days, Szechenyi is open for men or women every day of the week. If you're traveling on a budget, stop by Kiraly Baths where tickets are $5-

$10 as opposed to the usual $20 for most other baths.

While you're at the baths, get an aromatic massage or sweat out some toxins in the sauna. Some baths, like Rudas, even have their own bars or cafes. Don't forget to bring your waterproof phone case so you can capture the elaborate stained glass and sculptures common in many of the baths.

8. Go to an Outdoor Movie Screening

If you're visiting Budapest in the summer, you'll find no shortages of things to do in the city. One of the gems of summer are the outdoor English language movie screenings. At Budapest Rooftop Cinema you can see a mix of international, Hungarian, and English language films, while taking in panoramic views of the city. If you're interested in modern Hungarian cinema, check out Varkertmozi. Tickets usually run around $3, so this can be a good option for groups traveling on a budget.

9. Head to the Top of Buda Castle

Budapest is easily one of Europe's most picturesque cities. Spend some time taking in the views from the dome at the top of the Royal Palace at Buda Castle, where you can enjoy sweeping views of Parliament, the Danube, and the city.

Buda Castle sits on top of Buda Hill, which was the location of the residence of the Hungarian royal family dating back to the 13th century. Today the Baroque style Palace is one of Budapest's most iconic landmarks. The large, green roofed palace, sits at the top of the hill, overlooking the Danube. Most days you can see the Palace reflected in the water of the river. The Palace is especially stunning when illuminated at night.

It is also home to the Hungarian National Gallery, definitely worth a visit for their extensive collection of Hungarian art. The Hungarian National Gallery is especially notable for its portraits and Medieval art.

Bus 16 from Deak Ferenc ter takes you right to the top of Buda

Hill, at the doorsteps of the Royal Palace.

10. Visit Ruin Pubs

One of the most unique things about Budapest is its ruin pubs. Ruin pubs are a trend that started in the early 2000s when locals began building bars and restaurants in abandoned and dilapidated buildings.

Some places, like Mazel Tov, underwent extensive renovations, while some bars, like Grandio, kept their original grungy roots. At ruin pubs you can find dirt cheap drinks or some of Budapest's finest dining. Stop by Ankert for popular parties or Vintage Garden in the Jewish District for a glamorous meal.

"Budapest is a prime site for dreams: the East's exuberant vision of the West, the West's uneasy hallucination of the East. It is a dreamed-up city..."

M. John Harrison

Isabella Beham

11. Go to Szimpla During the Day

Szimpla Kert, on Kazinczy street in the Jewish District, is no doubt the most popular ruin pub in Budapest. At nights and on weekends, it's almost unbearably crowded, if you can even get in. Szimpla is definitely worth a stop though for it's cultural significance in Budapest and eclectic design.

Visit Szimpla in the late afternoon for dinner before it gets crowded. It's a great place for beer and cheap eats. Be sure to try their potato platter; it's literally a plate of potatoes cooked in several different ways. Once Szimpla starts to fill up, you can pop next door to explore their design store or cross the street for their coffee shop. If you are at Szimpla while it's busy, be sure to watch your bag. Pickpockets tend to target Szimpla as a place popular with tourists.

12. Go Hiking in Buda

When you're taking in the panoramic views of Budapest, no doubt you'll notice that the city is surrounded by scenic hills. Hiking in Buda is a great idea for an activity in the autumn when the weather is milder.

One of the more popular hikes is to Fairy Rock in the Buda Hills, where you can find excellent views of the city. If you're looking for a more leisurely pace, take an easy walk or chairlift to the top of Janos Hill, the highest point in Budapest. On the top of Janos Hills stands a beautiful lookout tower built around the turn of the 20th century.

13. Visit the Beach

With its sandy beaches and clear water, Lake Balaton is known as the "Hungarian Sea." You can reach the shores of Lake Balaton by car or public transit within 2-3 hours. Check out the beach village of Tihany on the northern shore for a historical town known for its lavender fields.

If Balaton is farther outside of Budapest than you want to go, visit Agard for a small beach town on Lake Velence, just 45 minutes outside of Budapest. Lupa Beach, also about 45 minutes away from Budapest by train is another nice option, but the lake is much smaller and you have to pay about $10 to get in. Once you get off at the train station you also have to take bus to get to the beach. Tickets to the beach by train are usually about $3 one way and leave every hour or more frequently in the warmer months.

14. Visit Romai

Romai is a beach on the Danube river, just 30 minutes outside of Budapest by train. If the weather is nice, you can also take the public transport boat there. It takes about an hour, but it's a great way to see the Danube and some of the sights on the river, like the Palace and Parliament for only a few dollars.

Romai is a great option if you're traveling with your family; enjoy their outdoor water park or let your dogs off of their leash by the water. For a more leisurely experience, you can also visit Romai's open air thermal baths. If you get hungry, you're in a great place to try traditional Hungarian street food like langos and fried fish. Be sure to bring cash with you though because all of the food stands will be cash only. Although most places in Budapest take cards, if you're leaving the city, it's a good idea in general to take cash with you.

15. Visit the National Szechenyi Library

The National Library is a great stop for the lover of literature. Founded in 1802 it is now home to over 8 million items including 2.5 million books and the oldest text written in the Hungarian language, the 12th century Funeral Sermon and Prayer. Make at stop at the national library if you're interested in learning about the rich Hungarian literary legacy. The National Library is also at the top of Buda Hill, in the same compound as Buda Castle, so be sure to stop by the library when you visit the Palace.

16. Go to the Night Baths

If you thought the baths were great, just wait until you've been at night. Rudas Bath has night bathing from 10 pm-4 am on Fridays and Saturdays. If you need a break from the hot baths, you can pop into the bar for a quick glass of wine before you head back into the healing waters.

During the summer months, Szechenyi has parties on Saturday nights from 10:30 pm-3 am, complete with a DJ and cocktails. During the winter the sparties, spa + parties, are held at Lukacs baths.

Night bathing on the weekends is the perfect way to unwind after a long week or relax your muscles after stressful travel. Walk back to your accommodations to take in the brisk air from the river after your warm soak.

17. Try Langos

If the sparties have left you feeling burnt out, langos may be the magical cure you need. Langos is a Hungarian street food made of fried dough. Traditionally, Langos is served with garlic, sour cream, and cheese, but you can get a whole host of toppings. Hot, doughy, and covered in cheese, langos is irresistible. Some might even say that it's better than pizza.

Langos stands dot the city from metro stops to Christmas markets. Although it may sound too heavy to eat in hot weather, it is also customary to eat langos at the beach.

18. Go Shopping on Andrassy Avenue

The most popular shopping area in Budapest is Andrassy Avenue, located conveniently right in the center of town, just a few minutes walk away from Deak Ferenc ter. Home to international luxury brands as well as local designers you can find everything from English language books to Swiss watches on Andrassy.
While you're shopping you can take a break at any of the great restaurants and cafes nearby. The Hungarian State Opera House is also located on Andrassy and the St. Stephen's Basilica is a five minute walk away, so some time spent combing the stores on Andrassy can be easily added to your schedule.

19. Get Brunch

Getting a hearty brunch is a great way to start any day of sightseeing. In the summer, locals love eating brunch outside at trendy restaurants.

Szimply, conveniently located downtown is a favorite. Visit Szimply for sinful french toast and a seasonally changing menu. Szimply is great for group travel because they always offer vegan and gluten-free options. Although their meals can be decadent, Szimply focuses on healthy foods and fresh produce.

Slow Foodiez, located in the popular area Oktogon, offers vegetarian interpretations of breakfast classics and power bowls. Stop by Slow Foodiez for a supercharged, healthy start to your day. If you're feeling adventurous, try their vegan omelette, made from chickpea flour.

If you've been traveling for awhile and are craving American breakfast fare, stop by Solinfo Cafe in the Jewish District for some homestyle pancakes. It's located right next to the Great

Synagogue, so you can make it your breakfast stop during your day of exploring the Jewish District.

20. Try Hungarian Cuisine

Trying the local cuisine is a great way to engage with the culture that you're visiting. Luckily, Hungarian food is filling, decadent, and inexpensive.

Langos and fried fish are great option for street food. You can find a street food market on Kazinczy street, right near Szimpla, called Karavan. Karavan is filled with innovative takes on traditional Hungarian and international street food. For modern classics, try Bors Gastro Bar, also on the bustling Kazinczy street. Bors is famous for their foot long, pressed sandwiches and creative soups. If you want to try something new, order one of their dessert soups or pork brain sandwiches. Don't worry, they do have vegetarian options too.

But to really sample local cuisine you have to have a sit down meal. Try Drum Cafe for the widest variety of Hungarian favorites. Hungary is famous for its goulash. Although goulash is popular in other parts of Central Europe, Hungarian goulash is special because of its use of sweet Hungarian paprika.

If you're vegan or vegetarian, no worries. You can try vegetarian interpretations of goulash at restaurants like Napfenyes and sometimes even Drum Cafe. Usually, these versions are made with beans instead of beef.

Once you have travelled, the voyage never ends, but is played out over and over again in the quietest chambers. The mind can never break off from the journey.

-Pat Conroy

Isabella Beham

21. Take in the Views from Rooftop Bars

One of the things travelers love the most about Budapest is its views. Take full advantage of this scenic city while you're here by heading up to Budapest's rooftops. Watch the sunset from one of Budapest's most popular bars, 360 Bar, named for its panoramic views of Budapest. From one side you can see the Basilica, the Parliament, and Buda Castle. Stop by 360 for dinner or drink. The best news is that the sun sets on the side with the best view, so be prepared to take stunning photos of the sunset and the Budapest skyline. Make sure to make reservations ahead of time at 360, which you can easily do on their website.

Unfortunately, 360 Bar doesn't usually take reservations in the summer months, and it can get pretty crowded. Luckily, there are a few other rooftop bars in Budapest. The luxurious High Note Skybar offers sweeping views of Budapest's major landmarks, while Liebling in the Jewish District has more of an artistic vibe and cheaper drinks.

22. Walk Across all of the Bridges

A great way to see Budapest is to give yourself a walking tour of the bridges. If you take a few hours to do this, not only will you see some incredible views of Budapest from the middle of the Danube, but you'll also see beautiful hidden gems in Buda and Pest, like the St. Gellert Statue and Waterfall at the end of Elizabeth Bridge (Erzsebet Hid). Start at Margaret Bridge (Margrit Hid) in the 13th district near Parliament. From there you can walk along the river seeing almost all of Budapest's major landmarks on the way.

Liberty Bridge, the green bridge near Gellert Thermal Baths, is a favorite spot for a romantic sunset among backpackers and locals alike. When the weather is nice, you'll see dozens gathered here to watch the sunset over the water every day. From this position you can also see Buda Hill and the Palace.

23. Visit Local Designers

Budapest has a thriving arts scene that would be a shame to ignore. Walking through Budapest you'll see the same brands you would see in any major European city, but you might also notice some unknown names.

If you're shopping on Andrassy Avenue you'll notice local designers like Nubu or Dorko. Stop by Nubu for high quality, minimalist looks or Dorko for contemporary streetwear. Also near Andrassy are Punch and the Garden Studio, delivering feminine clothing and accessories by local designers. Be sure to check out Anna Amelie handbags. If you're staying on the popular street Vaci utca, don't miss the luxury brand, Nanushka or the nearby Mono Art & Design.

If you're interested in traditional Hungarian designs, you should explore Romani. Romani captures traditional Hungarian/Roma culture in their colorful designs. They also serve as a pillar of the Roma community in Budapest, providing educational and career opportunities to disadvantaged women.

If you visit one of these stores, ask for a Budapest Design Map, a free map of Budapest that show where all of the local designers are.

24. Go to a Bar on the Danube

Between the thermal baths and beautiful sights, Budapest is an easy place to relax. Take full advantage of this by having an awesome cocktail on the river. Get strawberry margaritas and dinner at Esetleg Bisztro while you watch the sunset on the water. If you find yourself near the Palace or the Basilica, check out PONTOON. PONTOON is located just beneath the Chain Bridge, so it's a perfect place to end a day of sightseeing. Sip on froccs, Hungarian wine spritzer, in a hammock while you watch the boats sail by. Just on the other side of the bridge is Raqpart, another great outdoor bar. Eat dinner at Raqpart illuminated by the lights of the bridge and the Royal Palace.

25. Shop for Vintage Clothing

Budapest is filled with great vintage stores at bargain prices. A local favorite in Humana Vintage Butik in the Jewish District. Their prices change most days and can drop to 200 forint ($0.79) per item. Check their Facebook page regularly to see daily specials.

Humana has a great selection of items for men and women including incredible vintage dresses. If you find yourself caught in the rain or the weather is colder than you expected, Humana always has a great selection of trench coats, military jackets, and velvet blazers.

Szputnyik, also in the Jewish District, is another popular vintage store, although their prices aren't usually as good as Humana's. They offer their own designs as well as a vintage collection for men and women. Visit Szputnyik for quirky jewelry and vintage fur.

One of Budapest's best vintage stores is for sure Ludovika.

Unfortunately, they only sell women's fashions, but you can find everything from beaded slippers to stylish rompers. While you never know what you're going to find at Humana, the collections at Ludovika and Szputnyik are more curated.

There are also free maps of the vintage shops in Budapest floating around, so be sure to ask for one because they come with 10% off coupons.

26. Visit Gozsdu Udvar

Gozsdu Udvar is a covered pedestrian street located in the Jewish District, running perpendicular between the two popular party streets, Kiraly and Dob.

You can find everything on Gozsdu from a massage to an amazing meal. Visit 2 Spaghi for fresh, handmade pasta at a budget friendly price, or Jardin Bar for stunning vintage decor and gourmet cocktails.

Escape Rooms, live action games where you and your friends are locked in a room and have to figure out how to escape, have become popular all over the world. Most people don't know that escape rooms actually started in Budapest. Challenge yourself in an escape room before going dancing at Vicky Barcelona.

27. Explore the Jewish District

Before heading out for a night at Gozsdu Udvar, explore the cultural sights on the Jewish District, also known as the Party District, during the day.
If you're interested in Jewish history or the Holocaust, take a tour of the Jewish District and visit the Great Synagogue. Or try Israeli shakshuka at one of Budapest's trendiest restaurants, Mazel Tov. For those following a kosher diet, there are several strict kosher restaurants in this area, as as well as a kosher grocery store. Design enthusiasts will love the Jewish District, which hosts a number of great design shops. Check out Tom Dixon lighting designs at Solinfo Cafe or local fashion designers at the Velvet

Chemistry.

For a night out on the town, start with dinner in one of the best restaurants in the Jewish District. Vintage Garden is a beautiful French inspired restaurant, famous for its cocktails and stunning, feminine decor. Vintage Garden is a great choice for a romantic evening or a girl's night out. Pop next door afterwards for decadent desserts at the Sweet. If the weather's nice you could also grab a light dinner at Gozsdu Sky Terrace.

For a more low key affair, check out Epic Burger and Bar next to the Great Synagogue for spectacular drink deals and vegetarian friendly options. They have an extensive cocktail menu with favorites like passion fruit mojitos. One Sundays and Monday, all cocktails are just $3.50. Afterwards, head to Grandio Party Hostel just around the corner for an eclectic crowd of travelers and cheap brews.

28. Go on a River Cruise

Budapest is a popular port city for luxury river cruises. You might be visiting Budapest for this very reason. If not, no need to worry, you can still get the feeling of a river cruise in one night.

Take a day cruise down the river to see some of Budapest's best sights. Some "hop-on, hop-off" tickets include a river cruise and usually cost around $20. You can also buy individual day cruise tours for around $15-$20.

If you're looking to party, plenty of the popular party hostels in Budapest also have "booze cruises." Taking one of these tours is a great way to meet fellow travelers and see the sights illuminated at night.

For a more romantic experience, you can also find luxury dinner cruises on the Danube with multi-course meals and live music of your choosing. For a special occasion, you can even rent your own private boat.

29. Try Local Wines

Hungarians are proud of their wines, and for good reason. Parts of Hungarian wine country are actually within the same latitudinal range of France's top wine producing regions. Grapes grow naturally in Hungary; scientists have found a 30 million year old fossilized grape in a vineyard in Hungary.

Unfortunately, the communist systems of collectivization and mass production lower the quality of Hungarian wines. Before communism, Hungarian wine was widely consumed in royal courts and Hungarian oak was shipped to Italy and France to produce wine barrels. Today local winemakers are able to return to their roots. Be careful to avoid the cheap Hungarian wines that still flood the market though.

If you love white wines, try the famed Tokaji sweet white, from the Tokaj region of Hungary. Tokaj is a designated UNESCO World Heritage Site as the oldest wine producing region in the world. This region produced the first "noble rot" wine, today's Tokaji.

Noble Rot is a fungus that infects wine grapes and causes them to shrivel while retaining their sweetness, resulting in wines with an extremely high sugar content. Tokaji was beloved in royal courts, especially by King Louis XIV who called it "the king of wines and the wine of kings."

For red wine lovers, Hungary's sub-Mediterranean region, Villany, produces world renowned Cabernet Franc in its volcanic soils. Or try the spicy Egri Bikaver, "bull's blood," wine from the northern Eger region.

If you want to get out of Budapest for the day, take a tour of Hungarian wine country.

30. Take in the View from Fisherman's Bastion

Fisherman's Bastion is a look-out point built on Buda Hill at the turn of the 20th century in the neo-Gothic style. Its seven towers represent the seven Magyar tribes that invaded the Carpathian region in the 9th century. Today, Fisherman's Bastion is considered to be one of the best views in Budapest, granting a lookout point over Magrit Island, Parliament, the Danube, the city, and Gellert Hill.

Visitors love to take pictures overlooking the city from Fisherman's Bastion, so don't miss your chance to grab an iconic photo to commemorate your time in Budapest. Many hop-on, hop-off tours stop here, but if you're visiting the Palace, it's just a few minutes walk away, so don't forget to add it to your itinerary.

"Broad, wholesome, charitable views of men and things cannot be acquired by vegetating in one little corner of the earth all of one's lifetime."

– Mark Twain

31. Visit the Museum of Applied Arts

Admittedly, not all of the museums in Budapest are worth visiting; you should completely skip the National Museum. However, the Museum of Applied Arts, a 15 minute walk from the Great Hall, is an architectural wonder.

The museum was built by the Hungarian architect Odon Lechner at the end of the 19th century. Lechner brilliantly fused the trendy Art Nouveau style with Hindi, Mughal, and Islamic architecture, resulting in a truly unique building that is a work of art in and of itself. Its iconic green roof was designed with traditional Hungarian porcelain tiles, literally bringing all of these styles together under a Hungarian roof.

The museum's collection houses a diversity of artefacts from European furniture to Islamic art. If you're interested in Hungarian culture, the museum's Herend, traditional Hungarian porcelain, is out of this world.

The museum is perhaps most beloved for its white marble central hall, finished with beautiful stained glass and Islamic design elements. The Museum of Applied Arts is a favorite among locals as a location for events.

32. Catch a Performance at the Hungarian State Opera House

Just a few minutes walk from the Basilica and the city center, there's no excuse to miss this European gem. The Hungarian State Opera House (Magyar Állami Operaház) was built in 1875 in the neo-Renaissance style by a major Hungarian architect.
Today you can catch Hungarian opera and folk dance performances, as well as classics and modern Broadway hits.
Many performances have English as well as Hungarian subtitles. If you've come to Budapest for the Christmas markets, don't miss the Nutcracker at the Opera House to really get in the spirit.
If performances aren't for you or you just can't fit one into your

schedule, you should still visit the Opera House. Stop by for a guided tour or a quick cup of coffee in their cafe. After you've spent your day shopping on Andrassy Avenue, you could also consider having a glass of Hungarian wine and dinner at the Opera.

33. Take a Day Trip to Szentendre

There's a lot more to Hungary than just Budapest, so don't be afraid to get outside of the city for a day. An easy day trip you can take from Budapest is to the small town of Szentendre. Szentendre is about 45 minutes from Budapest by train. For $3 you can take a direct train to Szentendre that leaves from Budapest's Batthyany ter metro station. Instead of the train, athletic types can take a bike tour from Budapest to Szentendre.

If you're leaving Budapest in the spring, you'll be treated to views of the Danube along side fields of sunflowers and wildflowers. Travelers in the summer beware that not all of the trains of air conditioning, so get to the train early so you can grab a seat by the window.

Once you get to Szentendre, there's a lot to do. If you're interested in Hungarian crafts, you'll be able to find plenty of shops selling embroidery. Szentendre is also a great place to try Hungarian cuisine or langos.

On hot days, you might feel like getting in the water. Luckily, there's small beach where you can swim in the Danube or rent a small boat. If you have a sweet tooth, most visitor's favorite thing about Szentendre is the Szabo Marzipan Museum. The museum displays figurines, replicas, and works of art made entirely of marzipan. In their cafe you can sample marzipan and other sweets from their workshop. This is a great place to buy gifts to take home to your friends and family.

34. Try Hungarian Spirits

Unicum, a 200 year old herbal concoction, is Hungary's national drink. Today, it is produced by the Zwack family using their secret recipe calling for 40 different herbs. During the Communist Era, the Zwack family was forced to flee to the US and Unicum production was taken over by the state using a different recipe. After the fall of communism in Hungary, the Zwack family was able to return and resume production of Unicum, with the proper recipe. True Unicum is not sold in the US, so be sure to try it while you're in Hungary. You can even bring some bottles of this unique liqueur back to your friends.

Probably the more popular spirit is palinka, Hungarian fruit brandy. Hungarians have been making palinka out of plums, apricots, pear, really any fruit, since the Middle Ages. Palinka is described as being similar to an alcoholic jam and can be found in pretty much any bar in Budapest. As a rule it is only taken as a shot, not made into a cocktail, and locals tend to chase it with beer.

If you want to make an evening out of trying palinka, you can go to a palinka bar. Sample palinka at Zsindelyes Palinka House or pick up a bottle to take home with you from Magyar Palinka Haza.

35. Take the Public Boat

If you aren't willing to splurge on a river cruise, you can still have some fun on the river. The city of Budapest runs public transportation boats on the Danube. For less than three dollars, you can buy a ticket on one of these boats and cruise down the river and see all of the major sights like Buda Hill and Parliament. Whether you want to take the boat across the river to Buda, or want to take a long ride to Romai, public transport boats are a great option.

36. Get a Thai Massage

In seems like there's a Thai massage parlour on every corner in Budapest. If you're already loosened up from the thermal baths and all that palinka, why not unwind some more?

You can get a massage in Budapest for around $20 for an hour, sometimes even less depending on the type of massage. When we're on vacation, we're suppose to be recovering from the stress of work and everyday life. Massages in general are a great way to get cortisol, the stress hormone, out of your system for a healthy mind and immune system.

Thai massage is a 2,500 year old medical practice that has a similar effect as yoga on the body and mind. Thai massage is said to be excellent for chronic pain, stress, and headaches and from a spiritual perspective people claim to feel greater energy flow after a Thai massage. If you've never had a Thai massage before, take advantage of the cheap prices in Budapest to try one out. They might just become a habit.

37. Go "Dog Watching"

>TOURIST

You'll see dogs everywhere in Budapest, even restaurants. Hungary is world famous for it's unique dog breeds. You've probably seen pictures of them, but never seen one in person. If you hang out at a park in Hungary for long enough, one of these adorable pups might just show up.

The Vizsla is a Hungarian breed that's gaining popularity in the US because of their affectionate and sensitive personalities. Although they may act like giant laps dogs if you run into one in a cafe, they're actually one of the oldest hunting breeds in the world and can be seen depicted in ancient art work. With their short copper hair and loving golden eyes, you'll be able to pick a Vizslas out of a crowd.

Pulis are another breed you have to see. These "mophead" dogs were made famous by Mark Zuckerberg, who owns one named Beast. Pulis are another ancient breed, but they were used for herding and guarding, despite their small size. If you see a black, gray, or white dogs with long cords of hair flopping towards you, that's a Puli. Pulis are playful, intelligent, and friendly, but sometimes they can feel easily threatened, so approach with care.

38. Take an Architectural Tour

The architecture in Budapest is a uniquely beautiful mixture of European, Turkish, and Hungarian influences dating back hundreds of years. If you're interested in art history, communist architecture, or modern design you have to take a tour of Budapest's architecture.

While plenty of tours in Budapest will introduce you to some of its more famous architecture, if you want to find hidden gems check out KEK Contemporary Architecture Center. They run unique tours of Budapest exploring some lesser known beauties. Going on one of their tours is a must for photographers.

39. Stop for Coffee

>TOURIST

There's so much to do and see in Budapest, you're probably going to have to stop at some point to recharge, yourself and your phone. Luckily, Budapest is filled with excellent cafes for coffee lovers. If you're near the Basilica stop by Kavetarsasag, for modern, minimalist design. When you find yourself exploring near the Danube, head to Madal for what some say is the best coffee in Budapest. If you're looking for a glamorous experience or a great place for a romantic evening, check out New York Cafe for coffee and dessert in an ornate salon, or stop by for a dinner of Hungarian cuisine.

40. Get Dental Work Done

This one sounds a lot less fun, but getting dental work done in Hungary is one of Europe's best kept secrets. People from all over Europe fly to Hungary for inexpensive, but high quality dental work. In Hungary you can even gets surgeries, like wisdom teeth removal, for 10% the price of the US. If you don't have time for a full procedure, get your teeth professionally bleached for less than $30.

>TOURIST

"In Budapest, you'll find experiences like nothing else in Europe: Feel your stress ebb away as you soak in hundred-degree water, surrounded by opulent Baroque domes…and by Speedo- and bikini-clad Hungarians. Ogle some of Europe's most richly decorated interiors, which echo a proud little nation's bygone glory days."

-Rick Steves

41. Sit Outside at Deak

Budapest is cold for so much of the year, that when it finally gets warm out, it feels like the city is coming to life. One of the ways you can tell spring has finally sprung, is when the city puts up the ferris wheel in Erzsebet Park, just outside of the Deak Ferenc ter metro station.

To really live like a local, grab a blanket and buy a bottle of Hungarian wine or beer. Unlike the US, you can walk into a store and buy single bottles of beer. Head to Erzsebet Park to sit in the grass and enjoy the weather with hundreds of Hungarians.

The sunset and ferris wheel together make a truly scenic sunset. Deak Ferenc ter is right in the center of town, so whether you've been on Buda Hill or shopping on Andrassy Avenue, Deak is a great place to end your day.

42. Visit a Teahouse

If you need a place to kickback, but coffee isn't for you, you should check out one of Budapest's teahouses. They can be a great activity in the winter months when it's cold out or a place to spend some time working if you're a digital nomad.

Visit Altair Teahaz in the Palace District (ironically located nowhere near the Palace), about a 5 minute walk from the Great Synagogue. They have a vast array of gourmet teas for every kind of palate, but their specialty is their fruit teas. The interior is designed like a treehouse, so you can take your shoes off and climb up ladders to find a cozy little perch. For authentic Chinese teas, head over to Flying Bird Teahouse in the Jewish District.

43. Take a Free Walking Tour

One of the best ways to learn your way around a new city is to take a walking tour. Not only will you get great exercise, but what you can learn from a knowledgeable guide is truly priceless
Whether you're interested in street art or Jewish history, you can find a walking tour to accommodate your needs. The great thing about Budapest is that you can easily find individuals and companies that work for tips, rather than fees. Taking a free walking tour is a great option for groups traveling on a budget or those trying to pack a great deal of sightseeing into a short period of time.
Hungarians don't always have the friendliest service so check social media and with friends to find the best local tour guides.

44. Pay Your Respect at the Holocaust Memorials

There are several Holocaust memorials in Budapest, but a few stand out. Perhaps the most famous is the "Shoes on the Danube Bank." The sculpture memorializes a dark moment of Hungarian history, when members of the Hungarian Arrow Cross fascist party forced groups of Jewish people to remove their shoes, so they could later be sold, and face a firing squad on the banks of Danube river. The Arrow Cross shot and killed potentially up to 20,000 people this way.

Today there are iron cut outs of 30 pairs of men's, women's, and children's shoes on the banks of the Danube river, standing as a reminder of the absence caused by the atrocities of World War II. Visitors often bring flowers to decorate the memorial.

Liberty Square (Szabadság tér) is a fascinating park filled with monuments and memorials. The space is highly controversial for several reasons. For one, monuments to communism and democracy stand side by side. The Hungarian government is unable to remove the communist monuments due to a treaty with Russia.

In 2014, the Hungarian government erected a memorial essentially rejecting their responsibility in participating in the events of World War II. The memorial frames the Hungarian government as innocent victims of Nazi Germany and created tensions with the current German government.

To redirect attention to the victims of the Holocaust, activists, artists, and survivors started the "Living Memorial" also at Liberty Square. The memorial comprises of personal artefacts of survivors and victims of the Holocaust in Hungary, as well as tributes left by family members, citizens, and activists. The "Living Memorial" is particularly special because survivors and their families get to interact with and impact the way their experience is memorialized.

45. Buy a Map at Printa

Printa is one of the coolest studios on the Budapest arts scene. The unfortunate thing about most art is that it's too heavy or cumbersome to take it with you on an airplane, but Printa primarily produces screen prints that can be easily rolled up.

Printa is also popular for their simple clothing and handbag designs. If you're traveling with kids, they even have a miniature studio for children's clothing and art. However, the best thing Printa offers for visitors are their maps. Their maps are true works of art, beautifully printed with bright colors and unique illustrations.

The best part is that their maps were designed by their artists to highlight their favorite spots in Budapest, so if you want to check out local hotspots, grab one of Printa's maps for just $10. Once you've gotten all of the use you can out of your map of the thermal baths in Budapest, have it framed and hang it on your wall as a keepsake. Printa is conveniently located less than five minutes from the Great Synagogue, so purchase their map of the Jewish District before you explore the area.

46. Visit the Great Synagogue

Build in 1859, the Great Synagogue is unique because it's the largest functioning synagogue in Europe. The Synagogue is a one of a kind piece of architecture. Rather than taking inspiration from traditional Jewish architecture, the architects of the Great Synagogue were influenced by Islamic design as well as Europe's famous churches and cathedrals. The architecture of the synagogue reflects the culturally assimilated nature of the Hungarian Jewish community before the Second World War.

If you want to pay your respects to the sufferings of the Jewish community in Budapest, you should visit the memorials inside the Synagogue. Inside the garden there is a memorial to Raoul Wallenberg, who rescued members of the Jewish community by issuing fake visas from the Swedish Embassy. Wallenberg eventually went missing and died in a Soviet prison camp under mysterious circumstances.

The sculpture of the Weeping Willow tree that was made in his honor memorializes the Jewish lives that were lost in Budapest, while the stained glass behind it commemorates Wallenberg and other "Righteous Among the Nations" who did their best to save lives.

Attached to the Synagogue is the Jewish Museum featuring Jewish religious relics, including relics created by Jews surviving in the ghetto during the War, granting a compelling look into Jewish life during the Second World War.

47. Try Hungary's Birthday Cake

One of the most whimsical Hungarian traditions, is that of the Hungarian national birthday cake. Each year, bakeries across Hungary are invited to participate in a competition to create Hungary's birthday cake for the year, to be cut on St. Stephen's (Istvan's) Day, on August 20th.

For the rest of the year, bakeries across Hungary are encouraged to carry the birthday cake for all to try. Do a little research to see where you can find this year's cake in Budapest. Drum Cafe is usually a safe bet on where to find it.

48. Shop at the Great Market Hall (Vasarcsarnok)

A stop at the Great Market Hall is a great chance to try local Hungarian produce and buy traditional crafts. Hungary is famous for its paprika, so be sure to buy some special paprika paste to take home with you. Paprika paste is a Hungarian grandmother's secret to creamy sauces. Here you can also find Hungarian specialties like pickled peppers or other Eastern European classics like Balkan Ajvar, a sinfully delicious red pepper and eggplant spread.
The Great Market is covered, so if you've run into a rainy day, this can be a great place to spend an hour or two exploring. Each month, the Great Hall highlights the culture of on immigrant group present in Budapest. Find out which days are cultural days when you're visiting, so you can sample even more international cuisine.

The Great Market is located right at the end of Liberty Bridge, so feel free to add it to your tour of the bridges. It's also only a 15 minute walk from the Jewish District and Gellert Thermal Baths, so it won't be difficult to integrate a visit to Vasarcsarnok into your travel itinerary.

49. Try Traditional Hungarian Desserts

If Hungary's birthday cake gave you a taste for Hungarian sweets, you know that Hungarians know dessert. There are literally too many kinds of Hungarian dessert to list here. The Hungarian birthday cake might change every year, but there are some classics you just can't miss.

Similar to a strudel, retes may be Hungary's national dessert. Poppyseed, sour cherry, and sweet cheese are the most popular. Some people get all three at the same time because the flavors blend so well together. The key is to get them while they're hot, so go Strudel House to get some of the freshest retes in town.

Flodni is a traditional Jewish Hungarian cake popular at Christmas markets. It's essentially layers of filo dough stuffed with alternating layers of apple, walnut, poppyseed, and plum. If you're coming to Budapest for the Christmas markets, be sure to seek out this specialty for a flavor combination that can't be found anywhere else in the world.

You can find palacsinta at almost every Hungarian restaurant in Budapest. Palacsinta are essentially the Hungarian version of crepes, but they're stickier so they can handle more fillings. If you love the idea of chestnut's roasting on an open fire, try gesztenyepüré, a puree made from chestnuts, rum, and sugar, served with whipped cream on top.

Perhaps the most common Hungarian dessert though, is kürtőskalács, also known as chimney cake. These spiral dough cakes can be found, and smelled, on almost any street corner. Kürtőskalács is made by twisting dough around a rod, roasting it rotisserie style, then rolling it in toppings, most commonly sugar and cinnamon. At some places, you can even find kürtőskalács filled with ice cream.

50. Don't Do it All

It's literally impossible to do everything in Budapest, and with the casual Hungarian atmosphere, relaxation is the name of the game. So kickback and do what you can, because if you don't do everything you want, that's just an excuse to come back.

Visitors should be warned though that hostels are littered with tales of people who came to Budapest for "vacation" or "school" and never left. They're probably well on their way to visiting every bath and trying every flavor of retes.

At least come back to try next year's birthday cake.

Isabella Beham

Top Reasons to Book This Trip

- **Thermal Baths:** In the hot, healing waters your stresses will melt away.

- **Food:** Hungarian food is inexpensive, flavorful, and decadent.

- **Traditions:** Hungarians love their culture and they elevate it to a fine art.

Isabella Beham

> TOURIST

GREATER THAN A TOURIST

Visit GreaterThanATourist.com
http://GreaterThanATourist.com

Sign up for the Greater Than a Tourist Newsletter
http://eepurl.com/cxspyf

Follow us on Facebook:
https://www.facebook.com/GreaterThanATourist

Follow us on Pinterest:
http://pinterest.com/GreaterThanATourist

Follow us on Instagram:
http://Instagram.com/GreaterThanATourist

Isabella Beham

> TOURIST

GREATER THAN A TOURIST

Please leave your honest review of this book on Amazon and Goodreads. Thank you.

We appreciate your positive and negative feedback as we try to provide tourist guidance in their next trip from a local.

Our Story

Traveling is a passion of the "Greater than a Tourist" series creator. Lisa studied abroad in college, and for their honeymoon Lisa and her husband toured Europe. During her travels to Malta, an older man tried to give her some advice based on his own experience living on the island since he was a young boy. She was not sure if she should talk to the stranger but was interested in his advice. When traveling to some places she was wary to talk to locals because she was afraid that they weren't being genuine. Through her travels, Lisa learned how much locals had to share with tourists. Lisa created the "Greater Than a Tourist" book series to help connect people with locals. A topic that locals are very passionate about sharing.

Isabella Beham

Notes

Made in the USA
Middletown, DE
09 October 2017